ACKNOWLEDGMENTS

Thanks of course to my family and friends that put up with me snapping photos along theirs and my life's journeys.

For this trip in New York, a big thanks to John and Mary, of course my partner in life, Lynda. It was a great birthday!

~

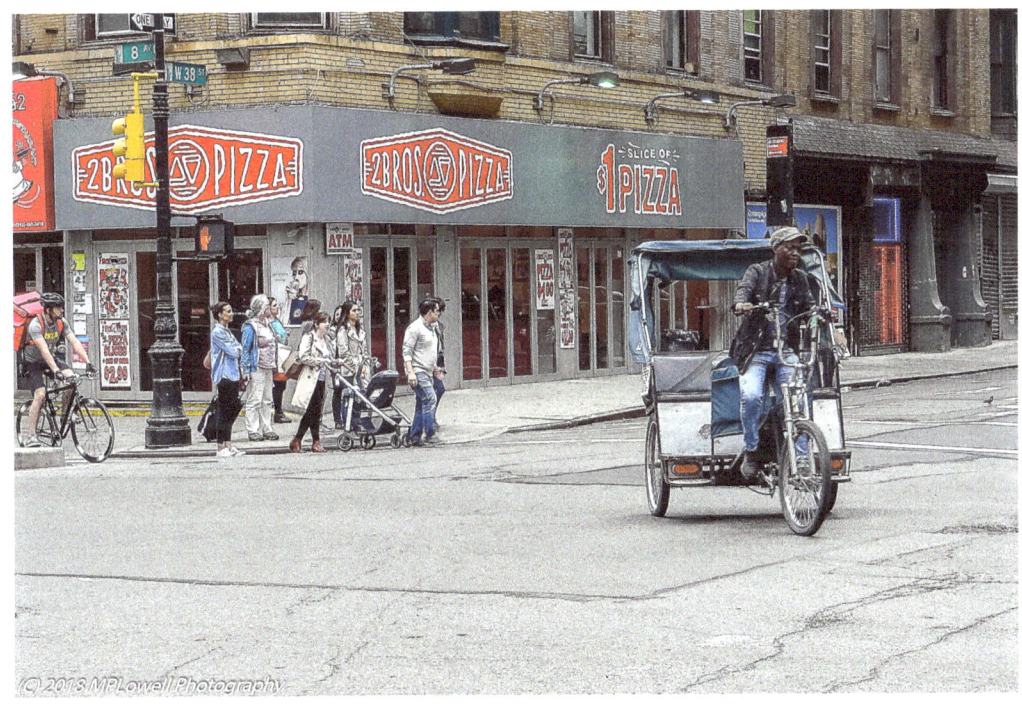
'Tourist Wheels'

MY WALKABOUT

Well, I did not start to write a book but hope you enjoy a new series I am creating called 'Bikes of...! I got the idea recently while on a birthday trip to New York City. Walking through the streets of Manhattan over a long weekend plus a day or two I began to see into the vibe of the street life of the city.

On the first few days I took the normal tourist photos and we saw many of the key sites around Manhattan but as we walk the city I began to see something else through my lens.

From Times Square, Central Park, Chelsea, Greenwich, Hell's Kitchen, Wall Street and countless other interesting places along our sightseeing I began to see the most interesting bikes. New, Old, Ancient, abandon, all types in all types of conditions and everywhere within the city.

From messengers speeding along to their next drop off to bikes abandon long ago these mechanical beings began to take on a life and tell thier stories if we just stopped and looked. It was fun to see the many 'walk's' of life these bikes have taken.

Hope you enjoy these images, maybe next time I'll be in your city.

M. P. Lowell

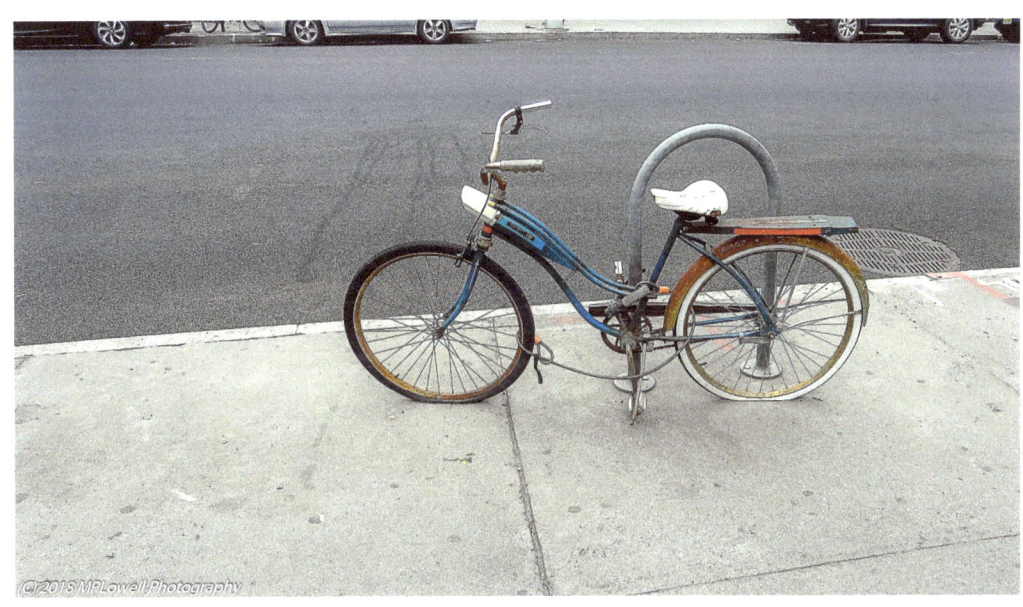
'Lonely Girl'

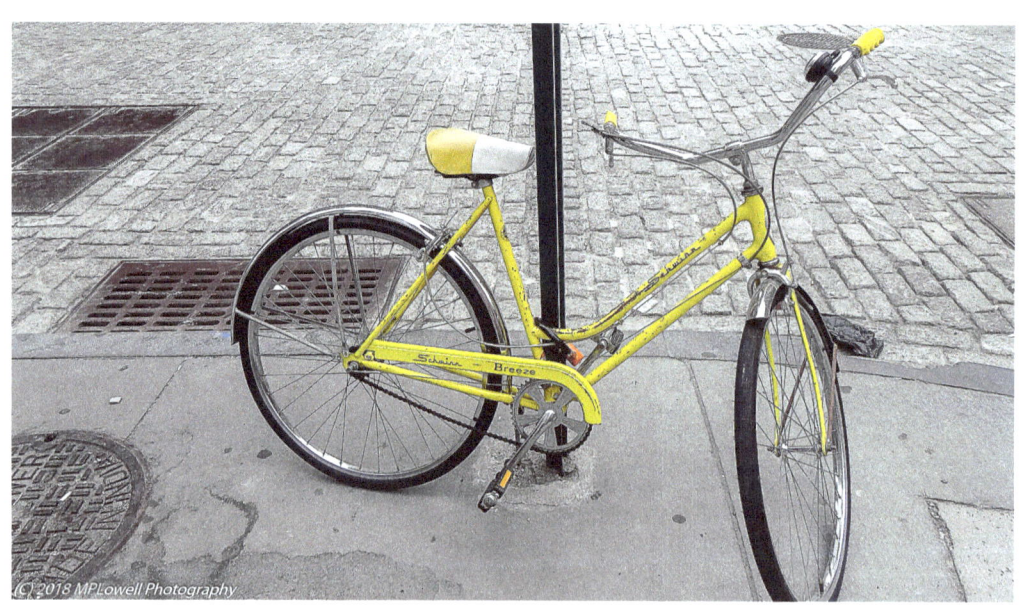

'Summer Breeze'

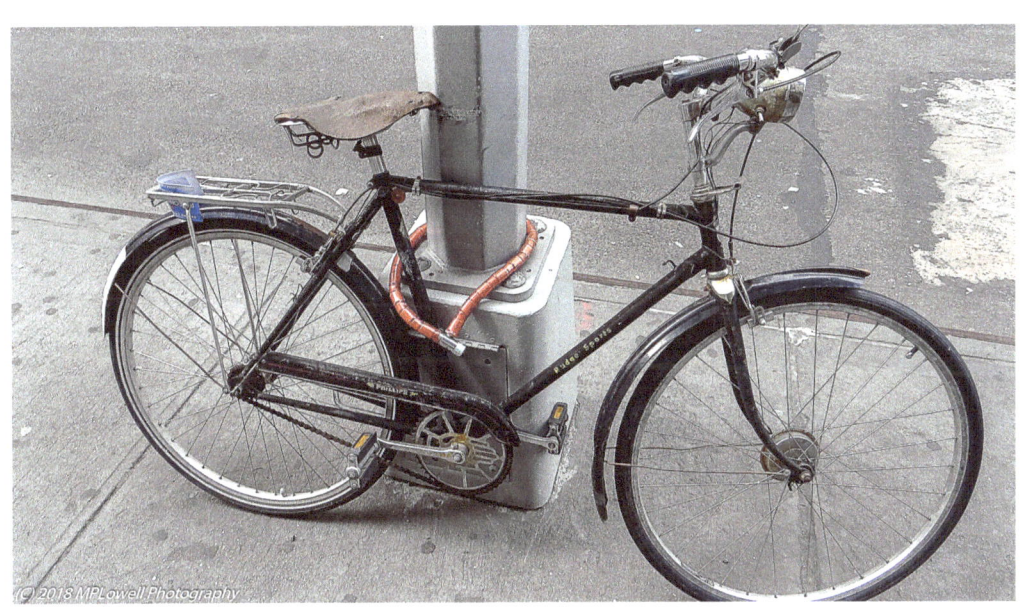

'Well Worn'

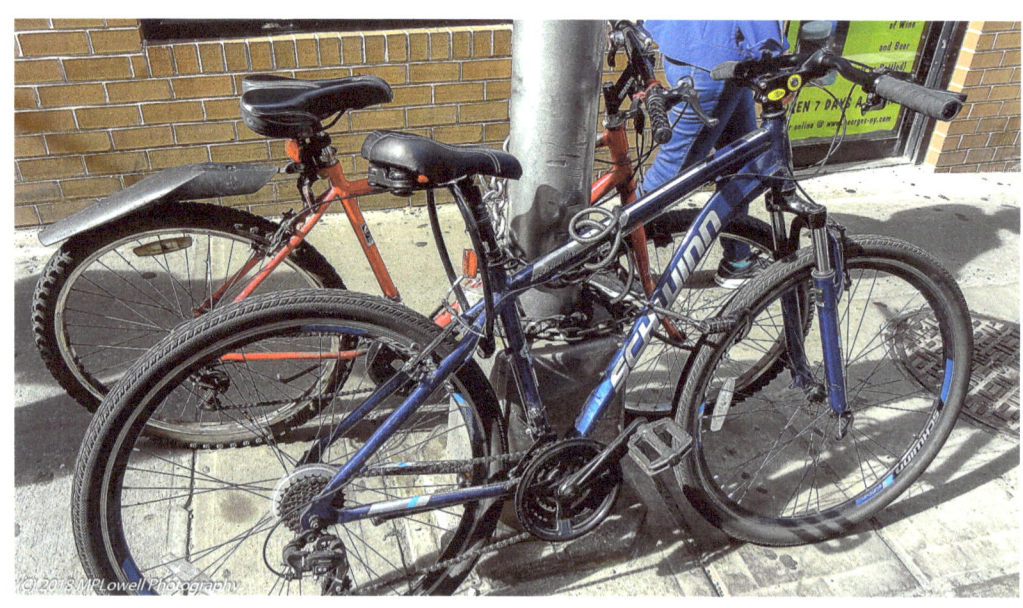

'City Trailers'

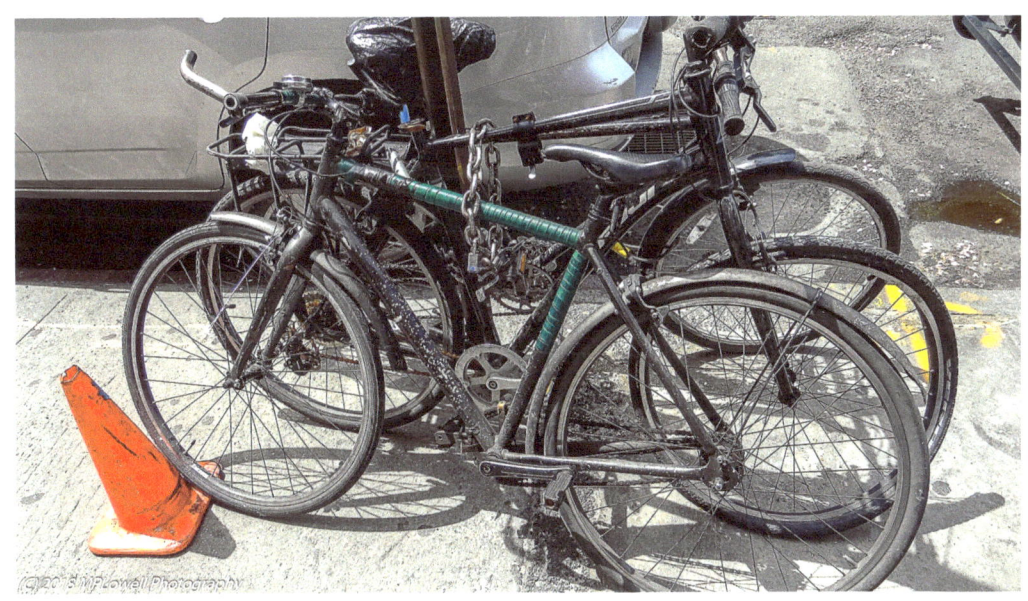

'Double Linked'

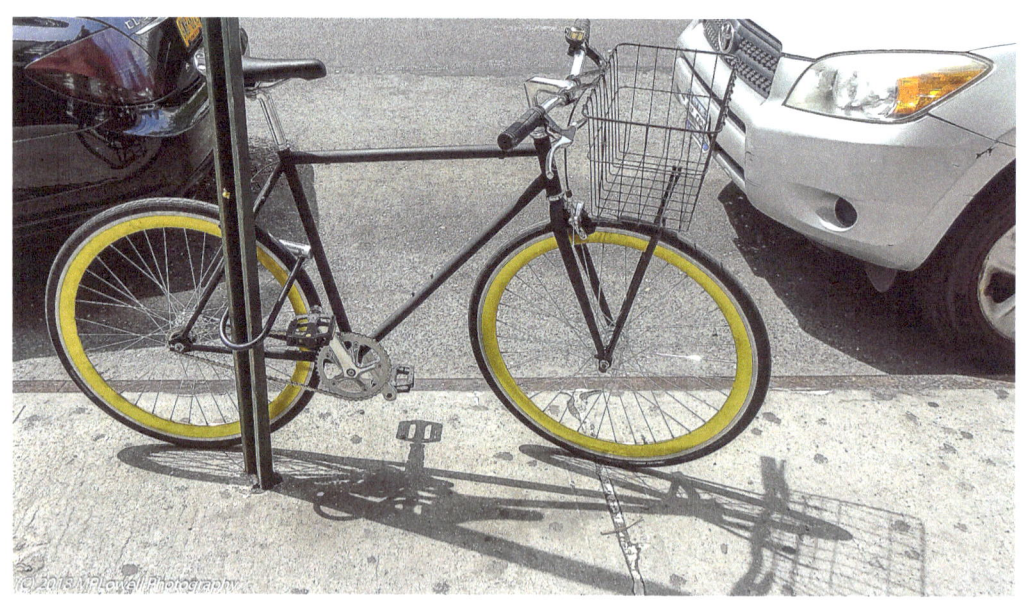

'Classy'

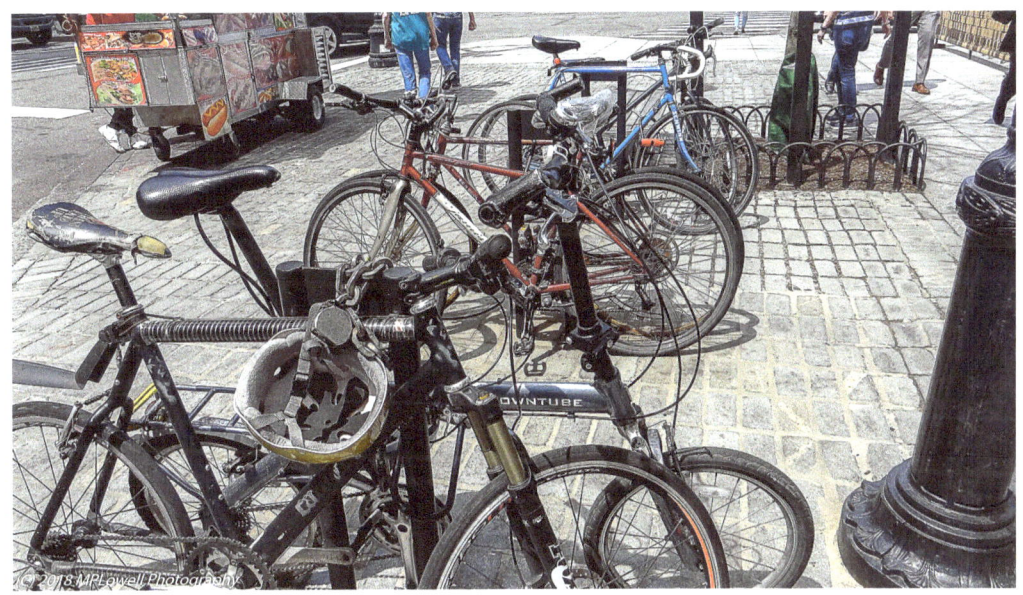

'Hitching Posts'

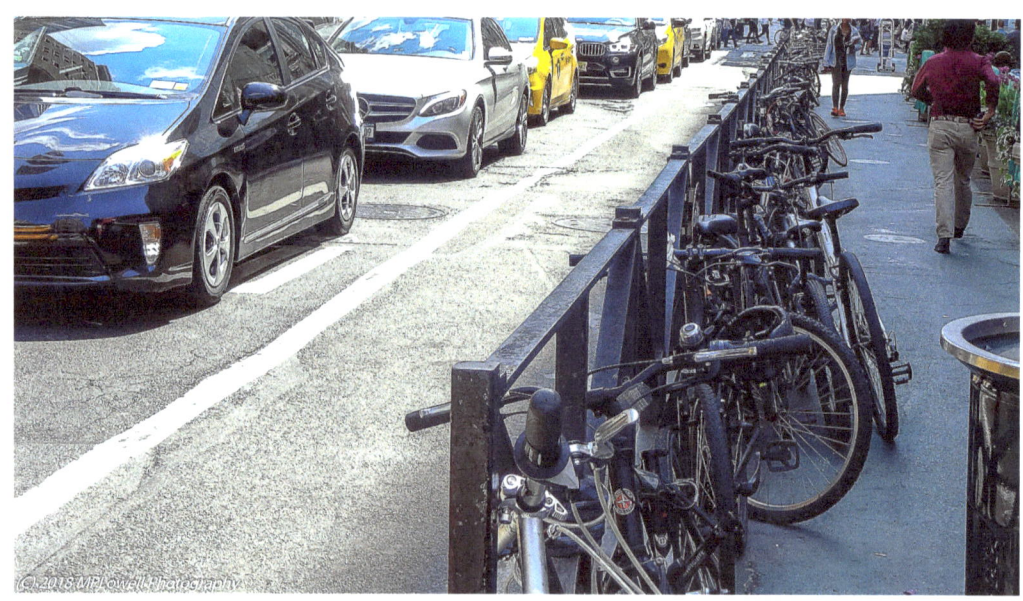

'Traffic Standing Still'

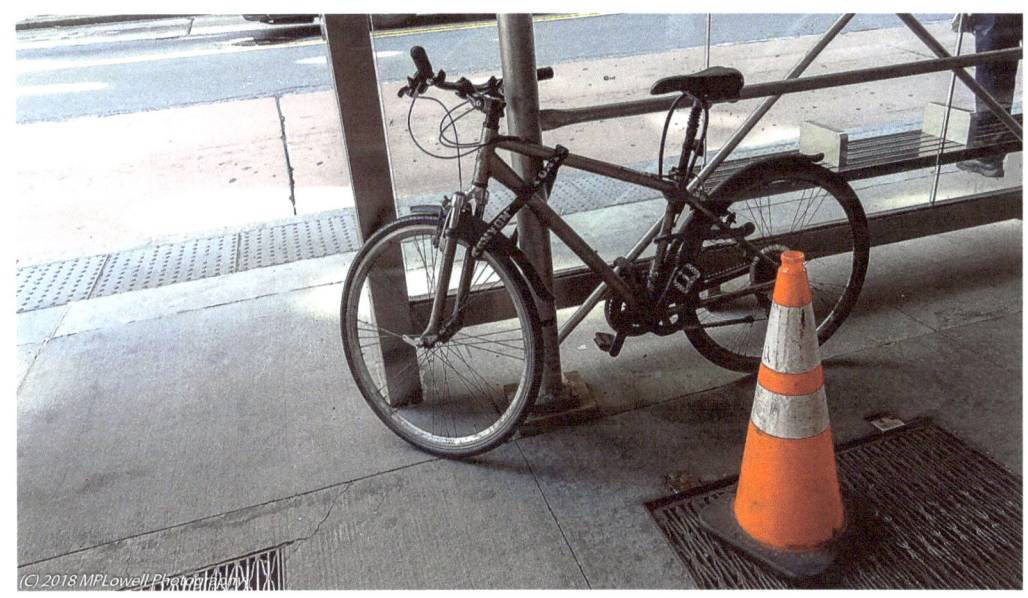

'Extra Precautions'

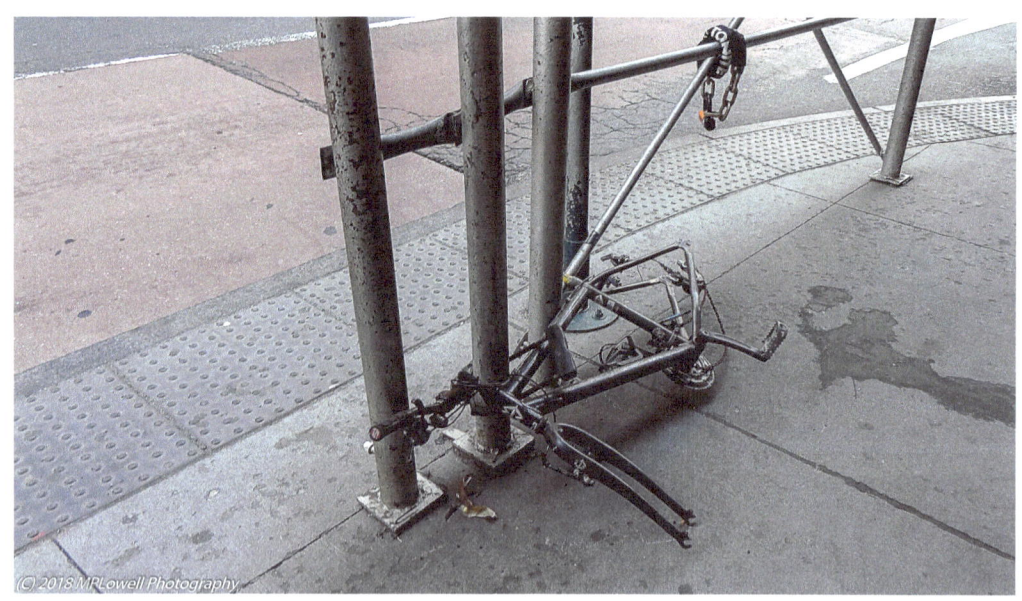

'Didn't Take Precautions'

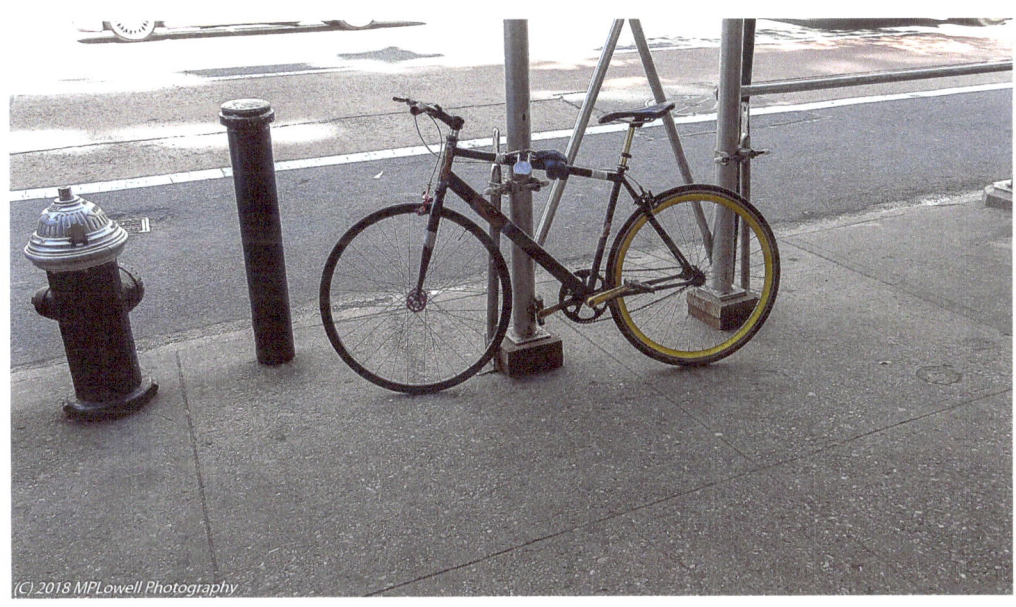

'Two Tone'

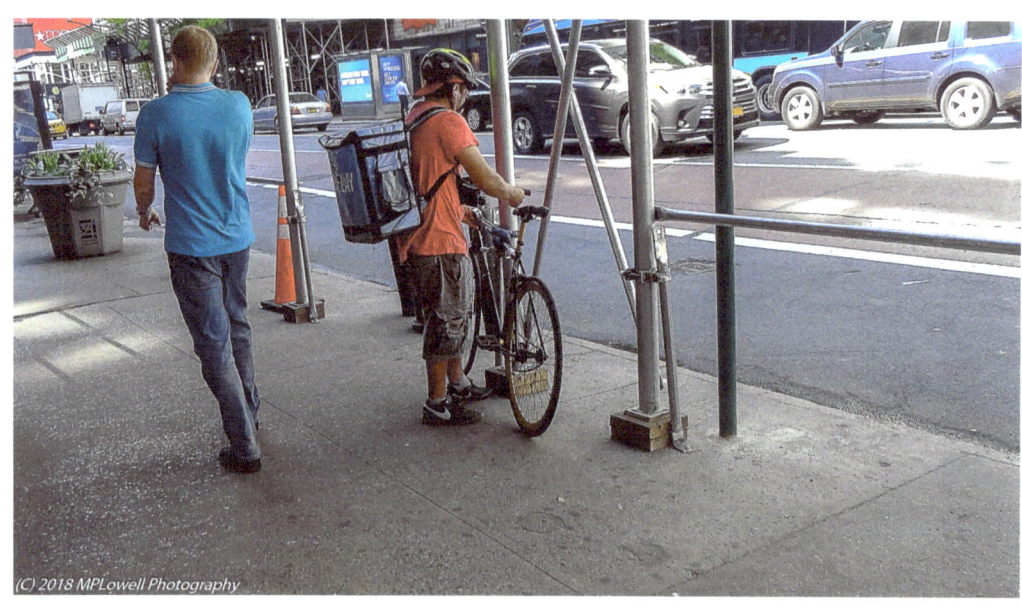

'Work Horse'

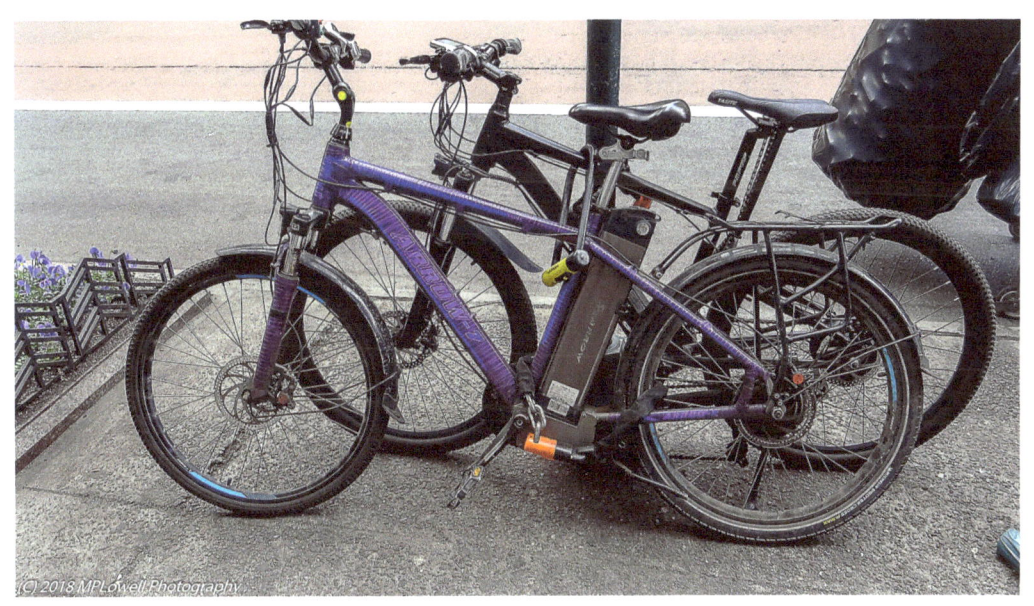

'Partners'

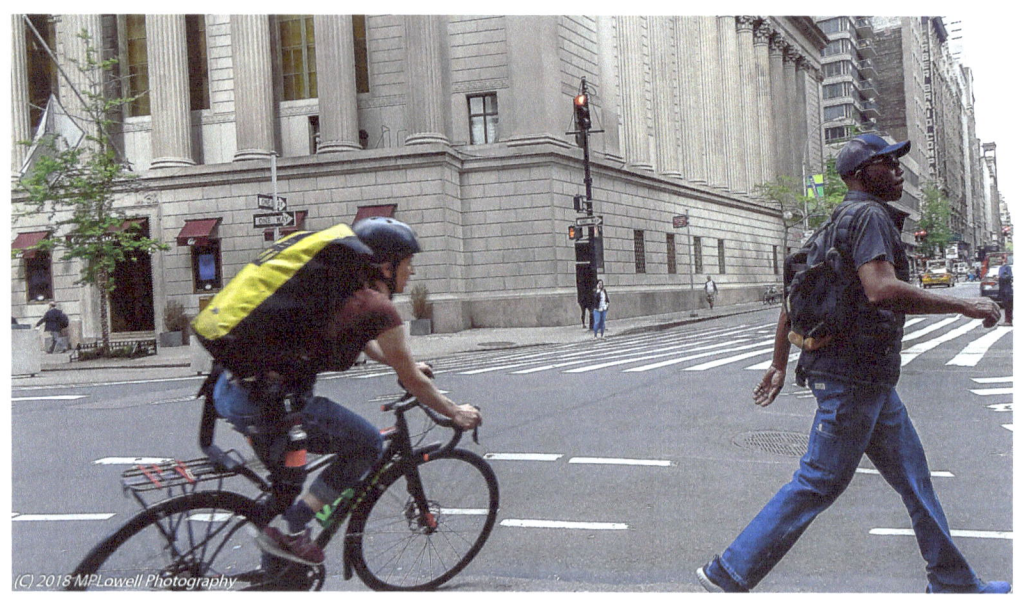

'Moving Fast'

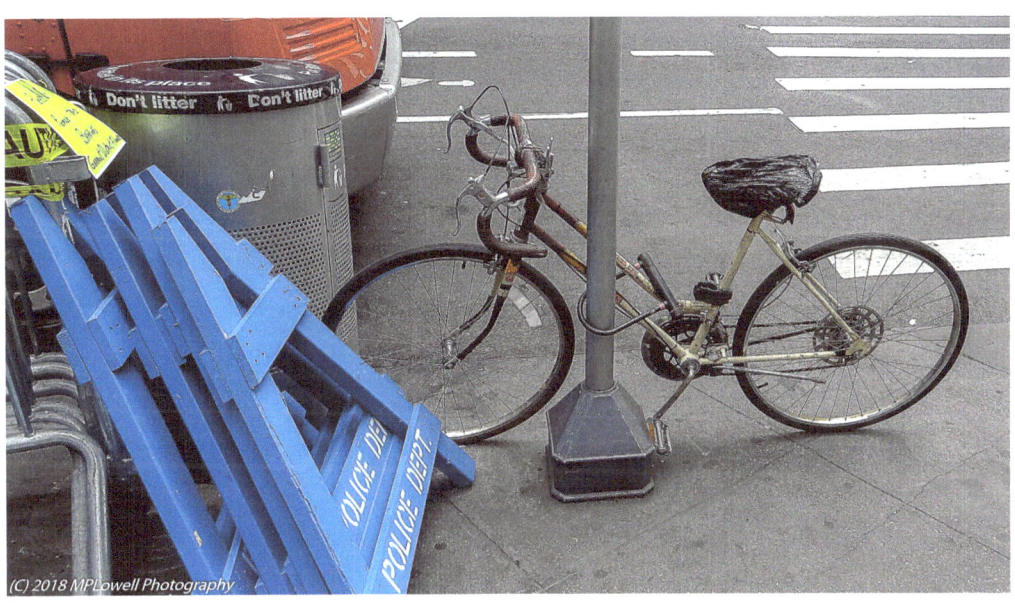

'No Parking Zone'

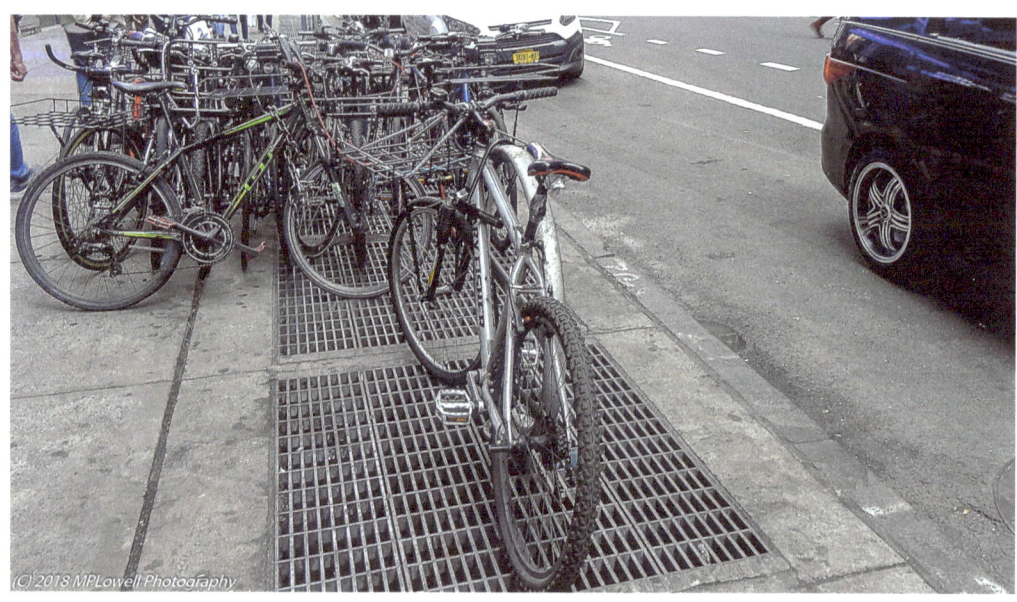

'The Leader'

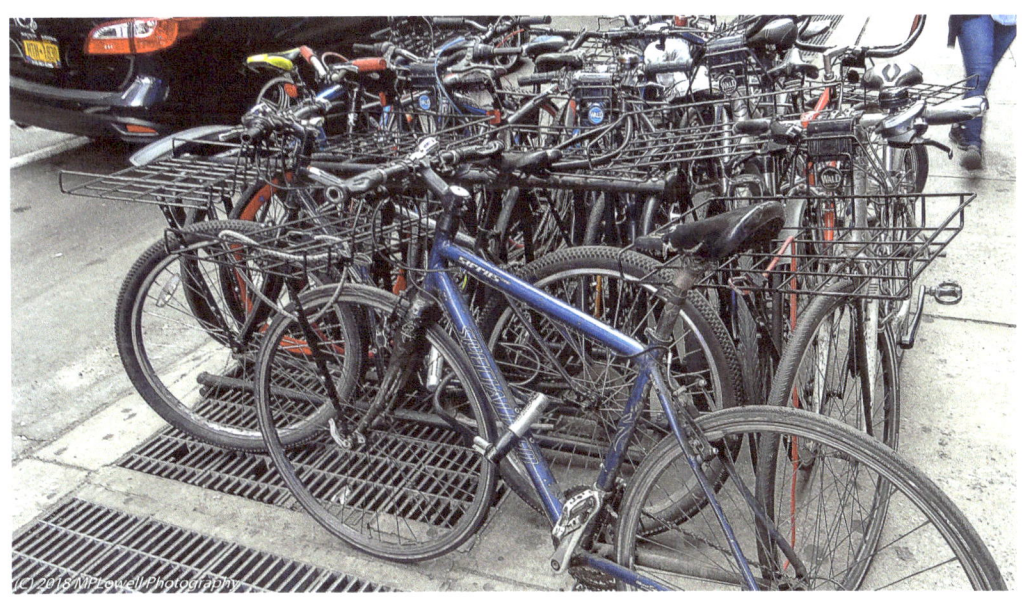

'The Pack'

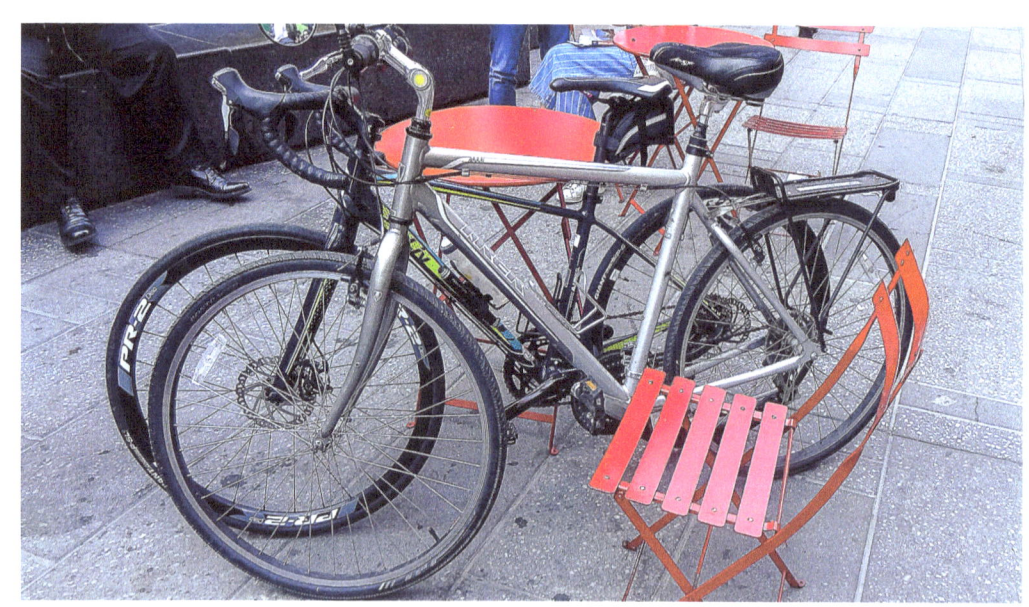

'Stopping to Rest'

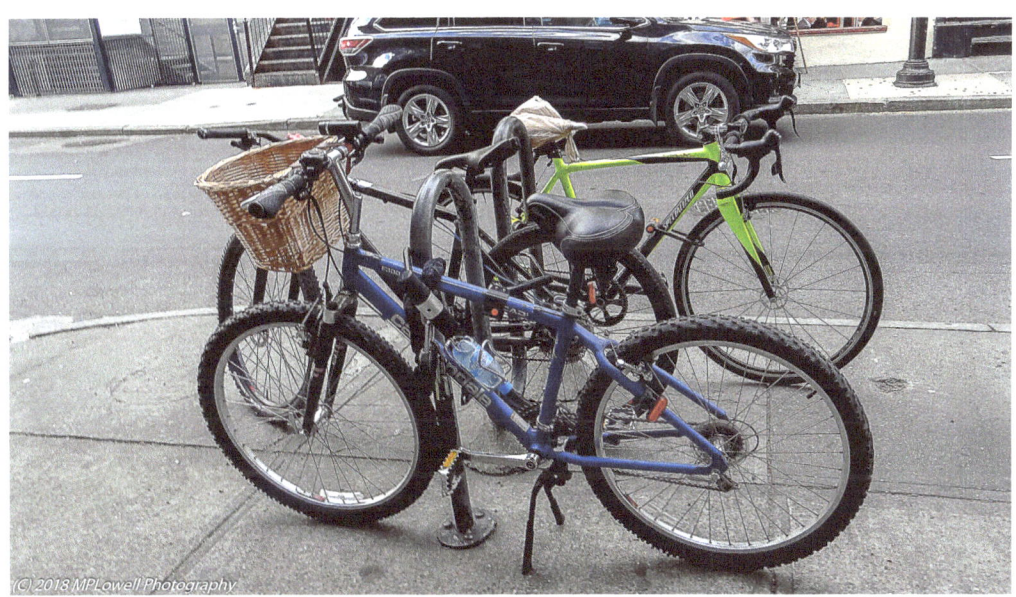

'Specialized!'

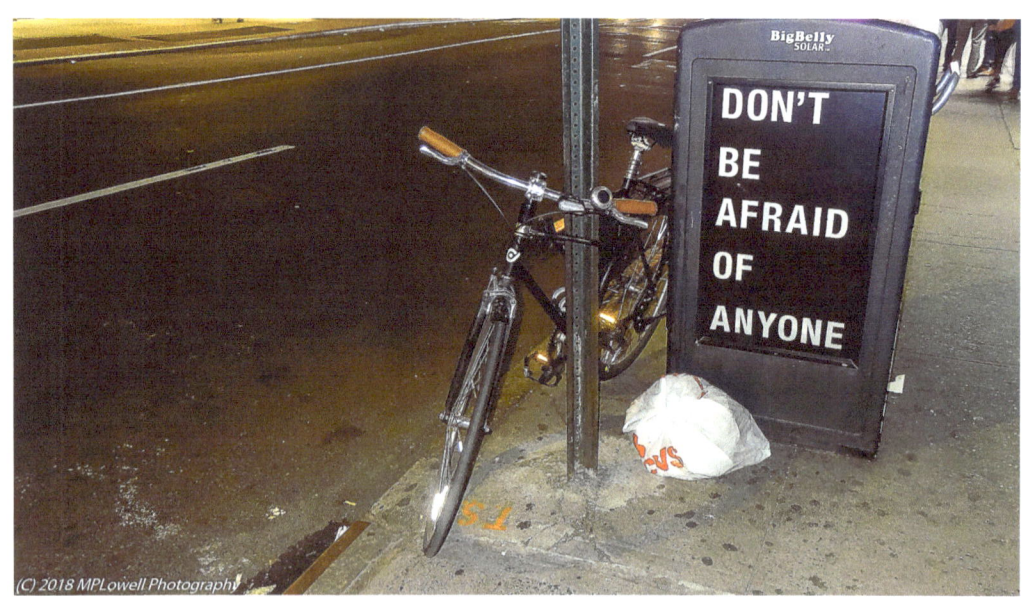

'Don't Be Afraid of Anyone!'

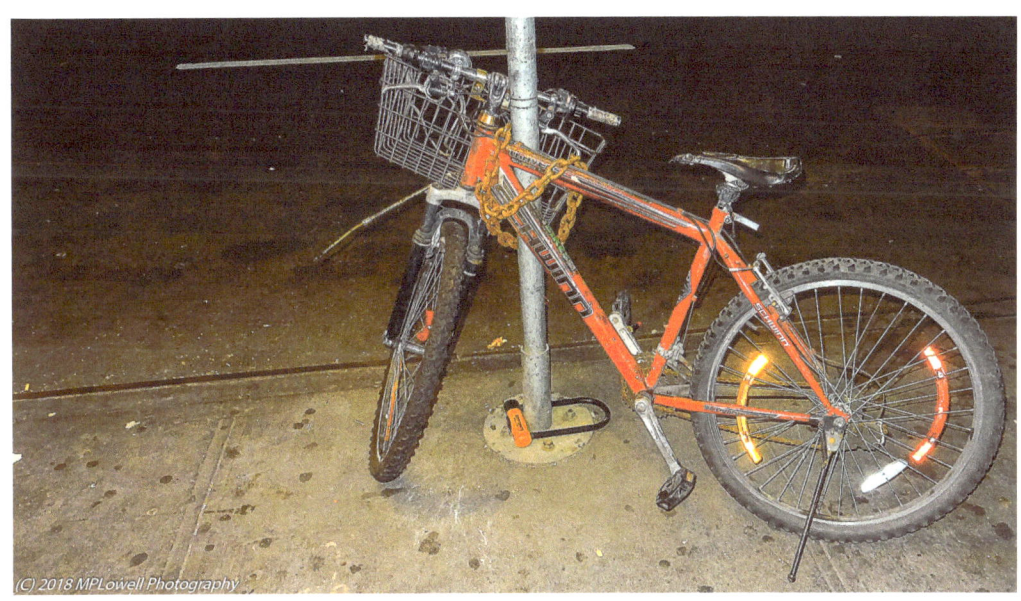

'Red Lightning'

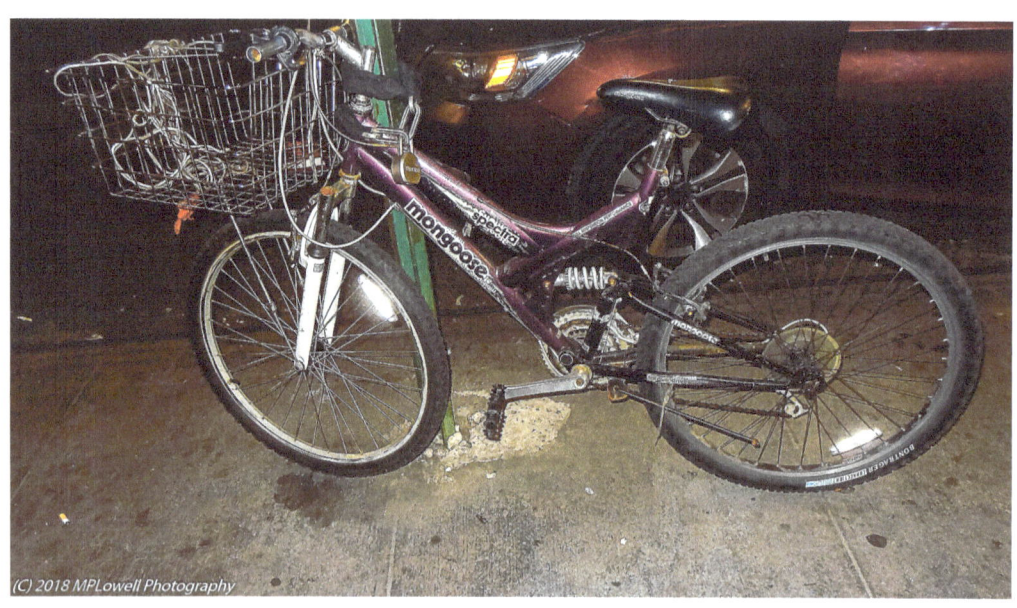

'Purple Nightime Mongoose'

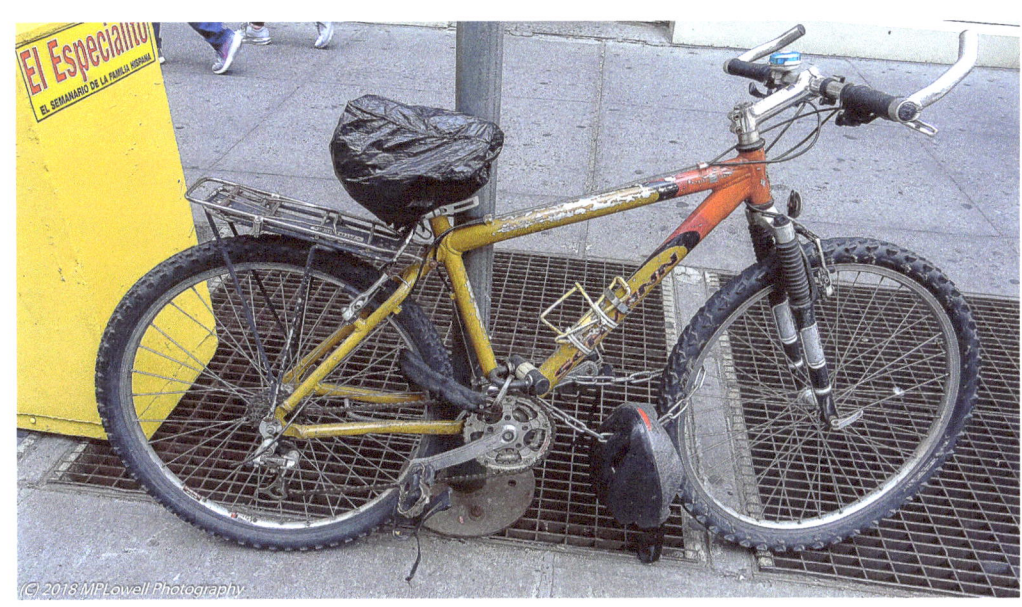

'Old Hand'

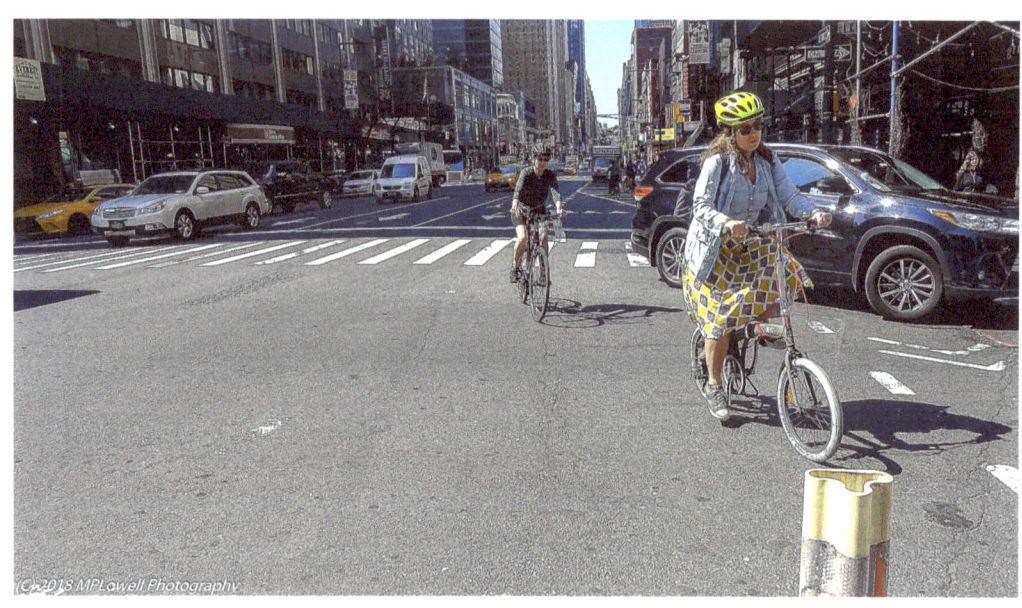

'New York Commuters'

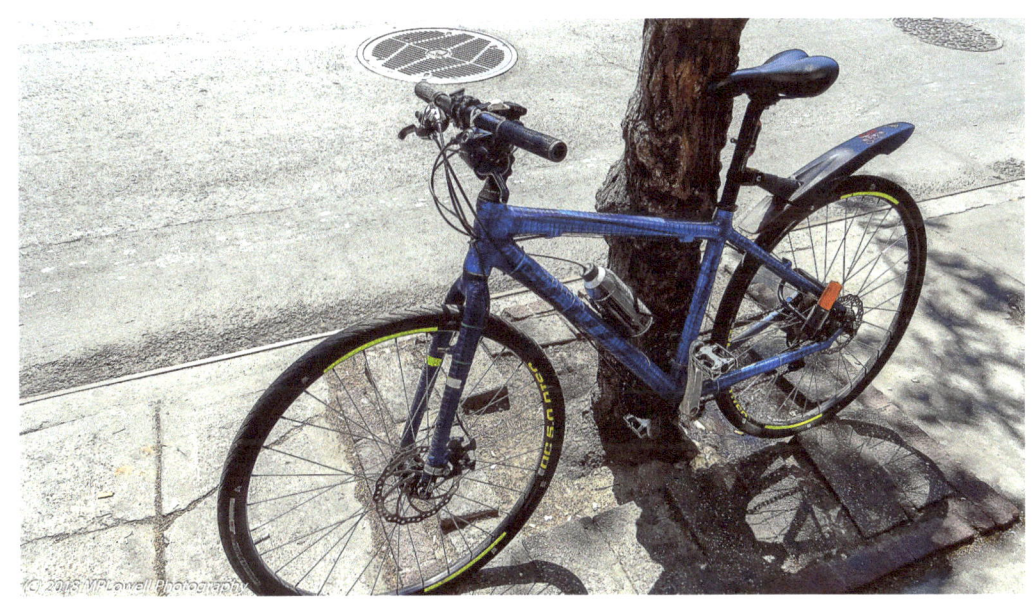

'New But Gone Soon'

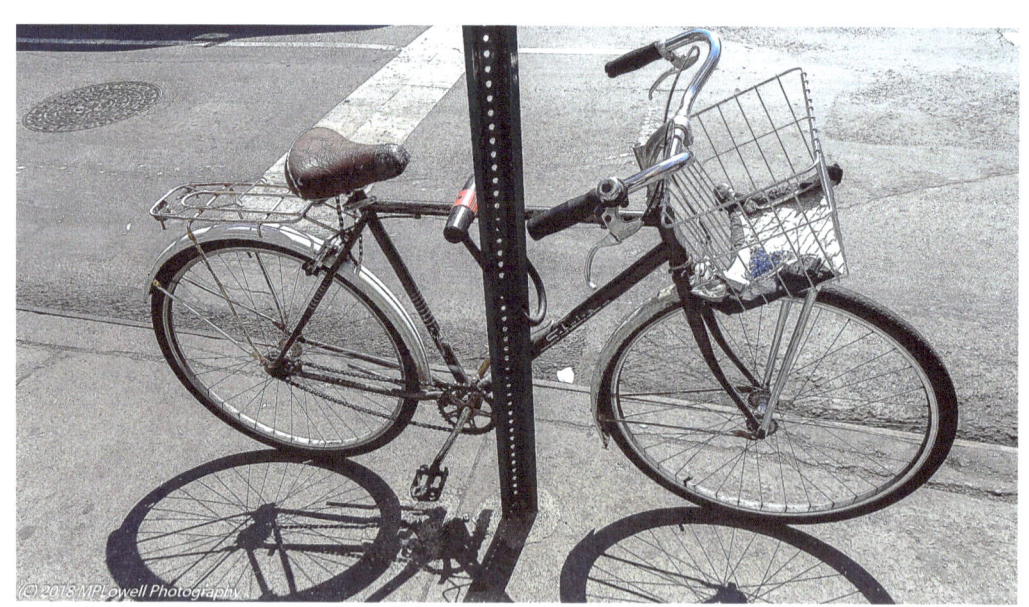

'Old Faithfull'

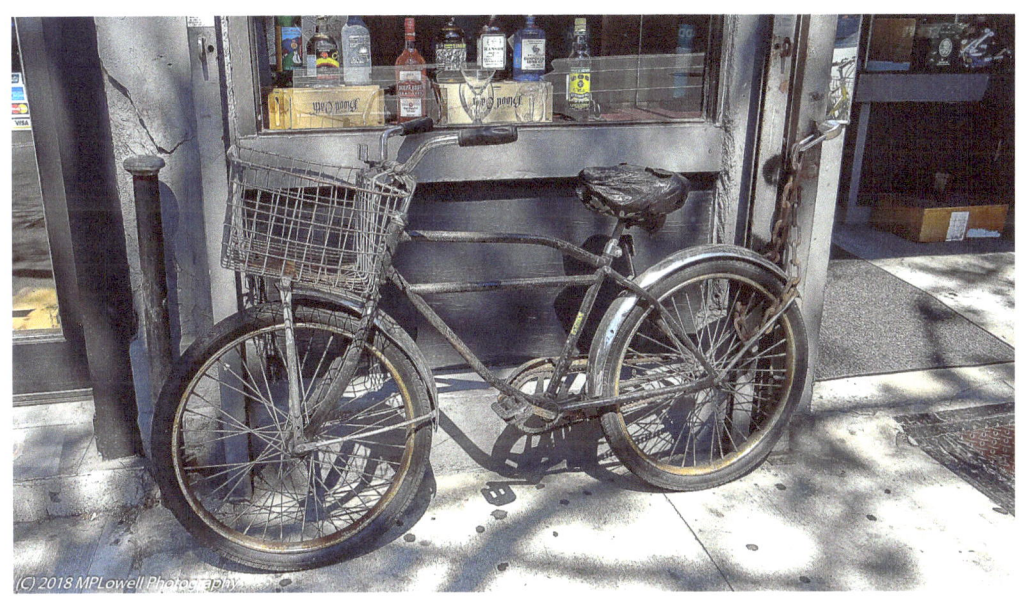

'Classic Oldie'

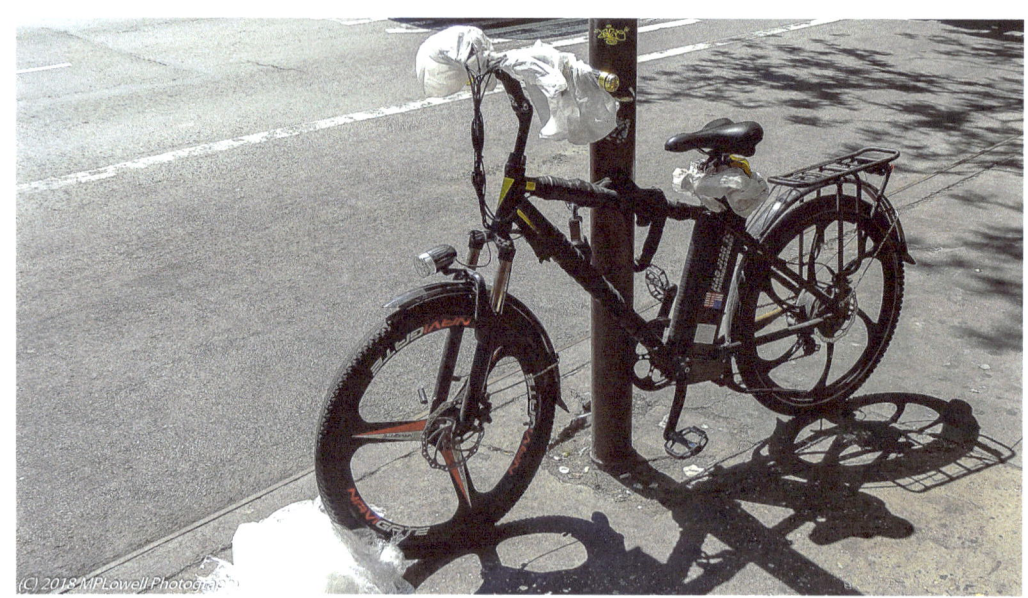

'Waterproofed'

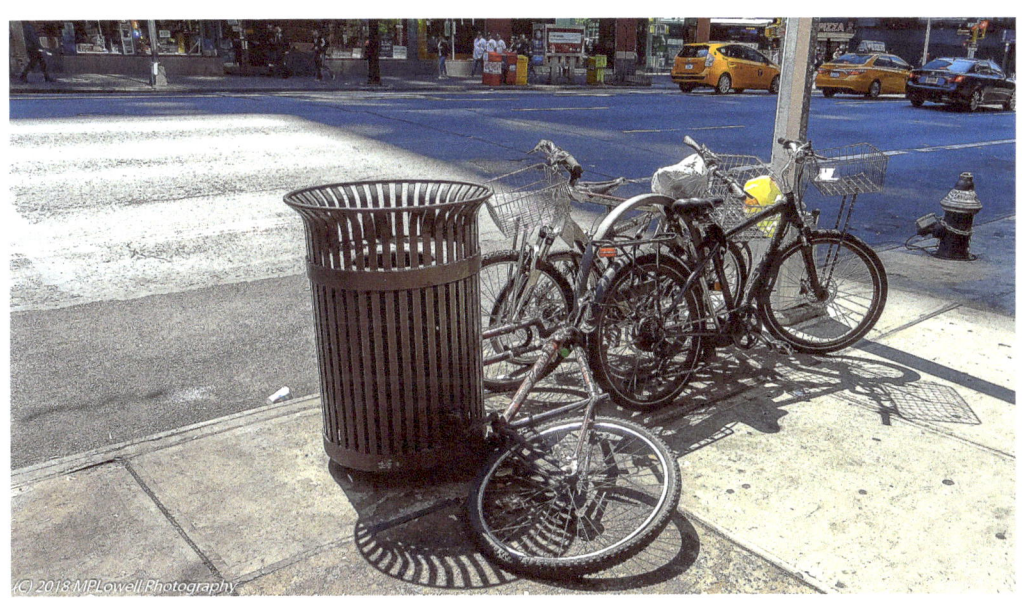

'Pile Up'

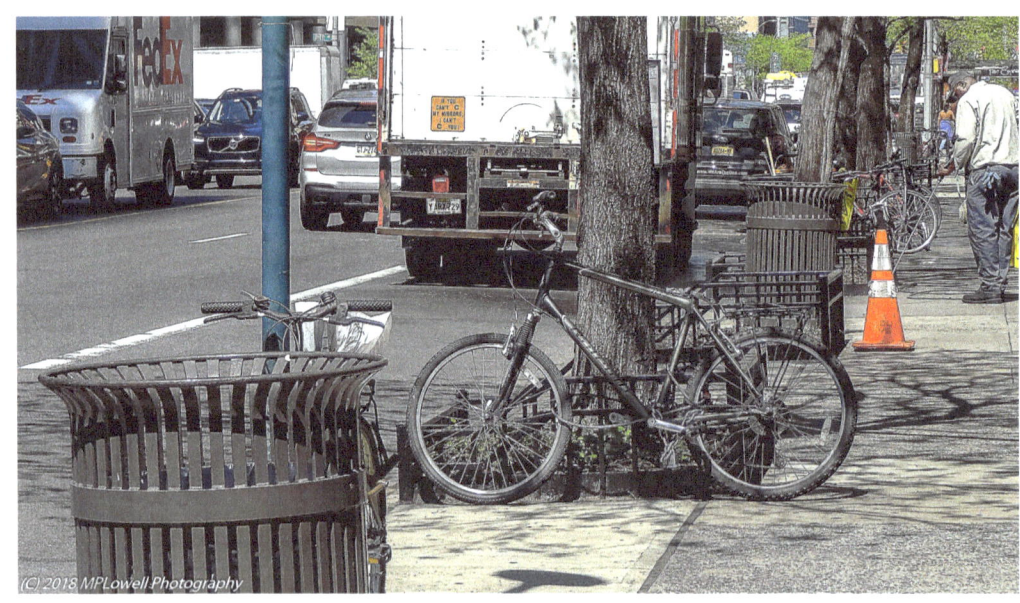

'No Place to Sit'

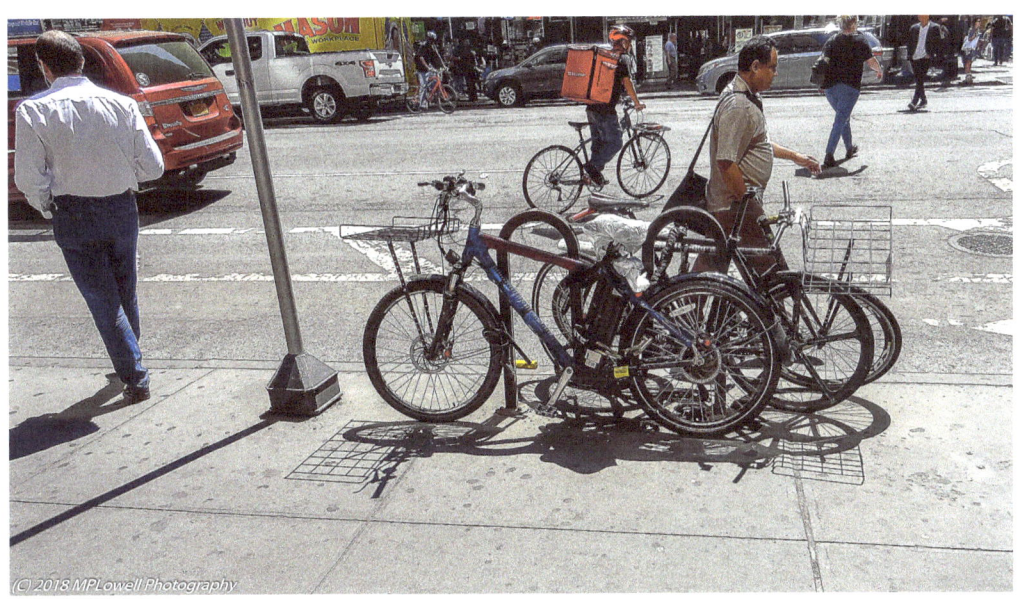

'Waiting for Riders'

The End

~

'Bikes of New York'

by

M. P. Lowell
@2018 MPLowell Photography
All Rights Reserved

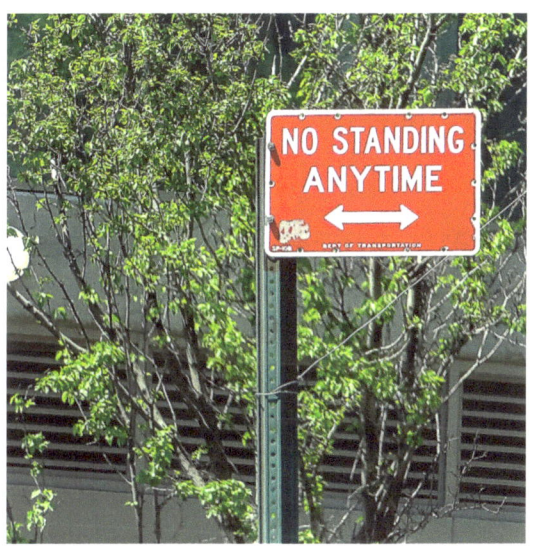

'No Standing'... 'Just Use Bikes!'

ABOUT THE AUTHOR

M. P. Lowell is a amature photographer, blogger and writer who loves traveling the world and experiencing life! Retired after a thirty-six year career in aviation, he is now making time for revisiting his favorite places and visiting new places to embrace the many cultures the world has to offer us all. He lives in the Pacific Northwest with his wife and family.

www.ingramcontent.com/pod-product-compliance
Lightning Source LLC
Chambersburg PA
CBHW040453220526

45473CB00004B/1622